SUNK !

Exploring Underwater Archaeology

SUNK!

Exploring Underwater Archaeology

Prepared by Geography Department

Runestone Press ◊ Minneapolis

RUNESTONE PRESS

rune (rōōn) *n* **1 a :** one of the earliest written alphabets used in northern Europe, dating back to A.D. 200; **b :** an alphabet character believed to have magic powers; **c :** a charm; **d :** an Old Norse or Finnish poem. **2 :** a poem or incantation of mysterious significance, often carved in stone.

Sunk! Exploring Underwater Archaeology is a fully revised and updated edition of *Introducing Underwater Archaeology,* a title previously published by Lerner Publications Company. The text is completely reset in 12/15 Albertus, and new photographs and captions have been added.

Thanks to Dr. Guy Gibbon, Department of Anthropology, University of Minnesota, and to Christopher F. Amer, Head, Underwater Archaeology Division, South Carolina Institute of Archaeology and Anthropology (SCIAA), for their help in preparing this book.

Words in **bold** type are listed in a glossary that starts on page 69.

Library of Congress Cataloging-in-Publication Data
Sunk!: exploring underwater archaeology / prepared by Geography Department, Runestone Press.
p. cm—(Buried Worlds)
Includes index.
ISBN 0-8225-3205-0 (lib. bdg.)
1. Underwater archaeology—Juvenile literature. [1. Underwater archaeology. 2. Shipwrecks.] I. Runestone Press. Geography Dept. II. Series.
CC77.U5S86 1994
930.1'028'04—dc20 93-42008
CIP
AC

Manufactured in the United States of America
1 2 3 4 5 6 - I/JR - 99 98 97 96 95 94

CONTENTS

ARCHAEOLOGY UNDERWATER

Archaeology is the science of finding, collecting, studying, and preserving objects from the past. Most **archaeologists** either dig in the earth for these artifacts or find them in the ruins of ancient buildings. But some archaeologists specialize in searching for objects buried underwater. These underwater—or maritime—archaeologists explore ancient shipwrecks, as well as buildings and harbors that have become submerged over time.

To search for remains under water, maritime archaeologists dive into deep seas and oceans. They face many difficulties and dangers on the seafloor. Murky water makes it hard to see clearly, and bulky underwater gear can impair movement. The water itself puts tremendous pressure on a diver's lungs. Without proper breathing equipment, underwater archaeologists easily suffer injuries. But by taking the proper precautions, archaeologists can safely explore the ocean floor for clues to the past.

The scientific methods used in underwater archaeology are only about 50 years old. The origins of this science, however, date to the nineteenth century, when **salvagers** were recovering cargo from recent shipwrecks. These workers—as well as professional divers who earned a living by searching for shells, pearls, and sponges (the skeletons of some marine animals)—often came across ancient **artifacts.**

An underwater archaeologist in the Florida Keys—an island group off the southern coast of Florida—points out the location of an eighteenth-century cannon on a site map.

Their finds soon attracted the attention of archaeologists.

Because archaeologists of the 1800s were usually not divers, they initially directed divers from the surface. These explorations most often took place in shallow water, where divers could see beneath the surface easily and could come up for air quickly. At that time, divers did not have special equipment to breathe underwater. Instead, divers held their breath while searching for artifacts. Eventually archaeologists learned diving skills and began exploring ancient underwater sites themselves.

Preservation and Destruction

A maritime archaeologist has one of the hardest jobs of any modern scientist. Working under water is uncomfortable, physically exhausting, and often dangerous. But the very obstacles that make underwater archaeology difficult, such as the depth of the sea and the coldness of the water, have helped to protect and preserve the remains of the past.

On land, ancient ruins are often out in the open, where wind, rain, and fire can destroy them. Even if objects have been covered by dirt

Not all underwater excavations involve searching for artifacts. This diving team from the 1930s prepares to recover the bones of a mastodon, the prehistoric ancestor of the elephant.

Ruins, such as this ancient settlement on the Greek island of Delos, can crumble from centuries of exposure to sun, wind, and rain. Sunken artifacts, however, are preserved by the cold, salty water of the sea.

over time, they are not always well protected. Organic materials—such as wood, leather, cloth, and paper—quickly rot and mix with the soil. Objects made of metal gradually rust when exposed to the air and water in soil.

The sea, on the other hand, protects artifacts. The saltiness of seas and oceans discourages the growth of **bacteria,** tiny organisms that can rot organic materials. Artifacts made of wood or leather, for instance, are preserved in saltwater. Metal objects buried in the nearly airless mud of the sea resist corro-

sion for hundreds or even thousands of years.

The fate of an object that falls into the sea mostly depends on where it lands. In some places, the artifact will be destroyed in days or weeks, while in other areas it may be preserved for centuries almost without damage. If an object falls near the shore, the action of waves will probably smash it to bits. But waves can also affect objects in deep water because the action is felt far below the surface. Waves that are 2 feet (.6 meters) high on the open ocean, for example, can

The action of waves can reach far beneath the surface of the water. Powerful ocean waves often break up and destroy ships and other remains resting on the seafloor.

grind objects that are up to 10 feet (3 m) below the surface. Much larger ocean waves are capable of destroying objects at depths of 50 feet (15 m) or more.

Animal Houses

Even if an object sinks below the action of waves, it is not always safe. If the item lands on submerged rocks, it will remain out in the open, vulnerable to destructive forces, such as ocean currents and sea animals. Some marine animals, including snails and worms, burrow inside objects, either to eat them or to find safe homes.

Other creatures—such as barnacles—cement themselves to the surfaces of submerged objects, giving the artifacts a crusty coating. The thickness of this type of crust depends on the temperature of the surrounding water. In cool water, the process of **encrustation** is slow. In warm water, small marine animals multiply rapidly. Even at depths of 100 feet (30 m) or more, objects submerged in the waters of warm seas can be quickly covered with a thick growth of coral. This rocklike substance forms from the skeletons of thousands of tiny sea creatures. Archaeologists once found a 300-year-old shipwreck covered with coral that was more than 3 feet (.9 m) thick.

Coral-encrusted artifacts sometimes rot within their hard cocoons. If the object is made of metal, it may rust away completely, leaving only a hollow space shaped like the object that was once inside. Archaeologists often use X rays to study encrusted objects. These invisible rays can pass through the encrustation to reveal the outline of an artifact.

A restorer removes a crusty layer from a bell.

Ancient Remains

Currents and marine animals cannot harm artifacts that sink into or are covered by deep layers of mud. As a result, archaeologists find many debris-covered remains in almost perfect condition. Ancient ships are often well preserved on the bottom of the sea, with their wood, ropes, masts, metal nails, and cargoes—even articles made of leather or cloth—still intact.

After many years under water, an ancient ship no longer holds its original shape. The weight of the vessel and its cargo gradually pushes the sides of the ship outward, until its framework sprawls on the bottom of the sea. In many cases, the collapse of a ship actually helps to preserve it. Once a ship is lying flat, it can become fully covered with sand and mud, which protect it from the destruction of waves, currents, and sea animals.

This eighteenth-century boat found in a river inlet near Charleston, South Carolina, was kept intact by surrounding mud and vegetation.

Looters and treasure hunters often destroy sunken ships to recover valuable objects, such as these silver dishes.

LOOTERS AND TREASURE HUNTERS

Underwater archaeologists excavate sunken ships to learn how seafaring people lived and worked in ancient times. These scientists carefully remove and study artifacts to ensure that as much information as possible is gathered about early peoples. But looters and treasure hunters can also reach sunken objects to keep as souvenirs or to sell.

Looters and treasure hunters focus only on bringing as many artifacts as possible to the surface. In the process, they destroy valuable information. For example, looters might damage the body of an early ship, preventing scientists from studying how ancient builders constructed the vessel.

In recent years, many museums have worked with underwater archaeologists to stop the destruction of sunken remains. These institutions have chosen not to purchase artifacts that were recovered by unscientific means or by people who intentionally damaged a site. By making the activities of looters and treasure hunters less profitable, scientists and museums hope important underwater archaeological sites will have a chance of surviving until they can be properly studied.

WORKING BENEATH THE SURFACE

Although the work of an underwater archaeologist is often exciting, it is also very slow and painstaking. These scientists need years of study and training before they can begin **excavating** (uncovering and recording) an underwater site.

During an excavation, the area of an ancient ruin must be thoroughly mapped out. Crews of workers must record the exact location of every object. Other specialists must handle the recovered artifacts with great care until they can be moved to a safe place. After excavation, archaeologists bring their finds to universities and museums where the artifacts are cleaned, labeled, photographed, and studied.

Diving Equipment

When archaeologists work beneath the surface, they wear special equipment to help them breathe, see, and remain warm. Most divers use **scuba** gear. *Scuba* stands for *Self-Contained Underwater Breathing Apparatus*. Scuba divers wear metal air tanks that hold compressed air or a mixture of breathing gases. These special breathing mixtures help to prevent injury to the lungs under water. Divers breathe air through a hose, which is attached to the tank and to a regulator that controls the flow of air. A pressure gauge, which is also connected to the tank, tells the diver how much air is left.

A school of fish swims past an underwater archaeologist.

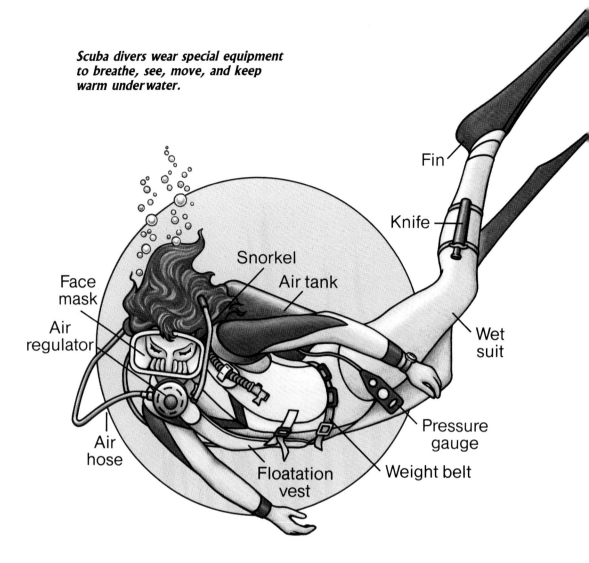

Scuba divers wear special equipment to breathe, see, move, and keep warm under water.

Fin

Knife

Snorkel

Air tank

Face mask

Air regulator

Wet suit

Air hose

Pressure gauge

Floatation vest

Weight belt

Scuba gear also includes a rubber wet suit, which keeps the diver warm in frigid underwater temperatures, and a glass-fronted face mask that allows the scientist to see clearly. A weight belt helps a diver sink, and a floatation vest can be inflated to help a diver quickly return to the surface. Fins, which divers wear on their feet to move easily underwater, are also standard equipment. But when very delicate work is under way, archaeologists often remove their fins to avoid damaging the artifacts and stirring up mud or sand that can make the water cloudy.

During excavations in very deep water, divers often wear thick helmets that cover the entire head as protection from water pressure. These deep-sea divers breathe with the aid of surface-supplied air or breathing gases. Surface boats use special pumps to feed compressed air through hoses to divers. On the other hand, divers swimming in very shallow areas use snorkels (short air tubes) to breathe air from just above the water's surface.

Surveying

To locate even a small site, underwater archaeologists often must explore a large area. They look for exposed objects that might be clues to the presence of more objects buried beneath the sand and mud. Archaeologists also draw detailed maps of the survey area, showing the location of natural features, such as vegetation, coral reefs, or underwater caves and cliffs.

On a muddy seabed, the water is often so cloudy that divers can see only 3 feet (1 m) or less in any direction. Divers move along at only about .5 miles (.8 kilometers) per hour. At a faster speed, surveyors might tire too quickly or miss seeing something important. In addition, diving time is limited by available air supply and water temperature. In very deep water, divers also need time to slowly ascend to the surface. Without this decompression time, divers can suffer harmful physical effects from breathing compressed air under water. Bad weather, which causes dangerous waves and currents, also can prevent surveyors from diving.

Between bad weather and cloudy water conditions, archaeologists sometimes are able to work on surveys only about one out of every

An archaeologist maps the location of remains that were discovered while examining a site.

Divers use scooter sleds—small, handheld motors—to quickly survey a large area.

17

three days. At this rate, an archaeologist working alone would need four years to survey 1 square mile (2.59 square km) of the sea bottom. For this reason, archaeologists have developed several techniques to make underwater surveying faster and more efficient.

The most common method is a **swimline,** in which several divers spaced a short distance apart swim together in the same direction. In this way, a large area can be thoroughly searched. Because a swimline requires many people and careful organization, archaeologists often substitute the faster **towed** **search** method. This technique involves towing one or more divers on boards—called sleds—behind a boat. Controls on the sleds allow divers being towed to look at the seafloor from the surface, stay at the surface or drop down to the bottom. On the surface, the boat's navigator uses floats or buoys to keep track of each area that has been inspected.

Archaeologists sometimes employ aerial photographers who can make detailed pictures of sites in shallow water. Surveyors also utilize magnetometers, instruments that find metal objects of all shapes and

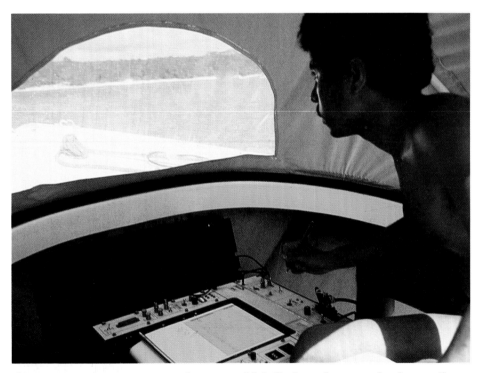

A surveyor operates sonar equipment, which finds sunken remains by sending sound waves through the water. Sonar, which comes from the beginning letters of the term sound navigation and ranging, was first developed by the British during World War I (1914–1918) to track enemy submarines.

sizes. **Sonar** is used to beam sound waves through the water. These waves bounce off solid objects and return as echoes, which can be processed by electronic equipment. The echoes are recorded as lines on a strip of paper that moves around a cylinder. After the survey is finished, scientists can study the paper to pinpoint where the echoes occurred. The readings reveal any large or unusual shapes on the ocean floor. Divers can then return to those spots to investigate further.

To search for sites in deep water, surveyors sometimes tow underwater cameras or ride in small submarines. In recent years, scientists

An archaeologist (above) working in the Aleutian Islands off the coast of Alaska lowers a small remotely operated vehicle (ROV) into the sea. Scientists control the ROV (right) from the surface.

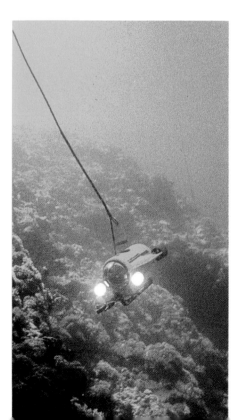

Workers lower an underwater vessel called a submersible and its crew of scientists into the Pacific Ocean. Although an average submersible dive lasts six to ten hours, this machine is capable of exploring the seafloor for up to three days.

have developed underwater robots called **remotely operated vehicles** (ROVs), which can explore regions where extreme cold, darkness, and underwater pressure have prevented human exploration. Some ROVs can operate almost 4 miles (6.5 km) beneath the surface. Most ROVs have cameras that send live pictures back to scientists on the surface, and some even have mechanical arms that collect samples from the ocean floor.

Excavating

Excavation is the process of scientifically uncovering a site by removing soil, plants, and rocks. In calm, shallow water, scientists can excavate a large area, moving downward layer by layer. In deep or rough water, archaeologists labor over small sections that must be rapidly excavated before heavy currents or the action of waves destroy their work.

On some excavations, workers install a grid (open, metal frames) above a site. A grid defines spaces for digging and is usually divided into squares called excavation units. In calm water, excavators often use rope to make a grid over a site. On land, stationary grids help archaeologists to map out a site, but underwater grids can be moved by the current or bumped by divers and therefore need to be constantly checked for accuracy.

During excavation, archaeologists must remove mud, rocks, and other debris from a site. In some instances, workers simply dump the **spoil** (excavated earth and rock) into excavation units that have already been excavated. But this method prevents archaeologists from seeing the entire site uncovered at one time.

The most common tool for removing spoil from an underwater site is the **airlift,** a device that

Using an airlift, a tool that works like an underwater vacuum cleaner, an archaeologist carefully removes spoil—sand, rocks, and vegetation—from a find.

sucks up the soil through a long tube. The tube is connected to an air compressor on the dive boat. Air rising in the tube expands, causing soil near the tube's lower end to be sucked up. The airlift is handled by two excavators. One person holds the lower end of the tube above the area that needs to be cleared. The other worker watches the spoil for artifacts that may have been missed by the first excavator. Other workers discharge the spoil away from the site.

When excavators recover objects that are encrusted with coral or lodged under rocks, they use tools such as hammers, picks, and crowbars to chip away the spoil. In some cases, workers even set off underwater explosives to break up very hard formations. This method is very dangerous, however. Some excavations require the use of an underwater chain saw. For example, large ships that are too big to be recovered in one piece are sometimes cut into sections before being brought to the surface.

The Underwater Record

In the early days of underwater archaeology, the emphasis was on recovering objects. The idea was to quickly haul as much as possible to the surface, clean the objects that were found, and display them as curiosities in museums. As the

Excavators use ropes and metal grids to divide a site into sections. Firmly anchored grids help archaeologists chart the specific location of each artifact.

Two divers measure a site while a third uses a special underwater pen to record the data on plastic sheets.

Workers use ropes and pulleys to haul the wheel of an ancient ship aboard a surface support boat.

science of maritime archaeology developed, however, it became clear that much could be learned from a ruin or a shipwreck by carefully studying the remains before removing them from the water.

Sometimes, for example, it is important to know which objects were on top of a pile and which were on the bottom. The direction in which an artifact was facing could also have meaning. This information may not seem important during the excavation, but the data may later provide clues about how and when a shipwreck occurred. For this reason, archaeologists now take photographs, make drawings, and record the location of each object excavated. If these details are not recorded before the wreck is taken apart, the information could be lost forever.

To note the location of each artifact, as well as other data about the site, some excavators write on clear plastic pages. These pages are clipped or taped to small boards, and special pencils and markers are attached to the boards with string. Other recording tools tied to the clipboard include rulers, compasses, and depth gauges (devices that measure the depth of different parts of a site). Some archaeologists speak into underwater tape recorders or use diver-to-surface communications systems to relate details.

Excavators use a variety of methods to remove ancient artifacts. Some divers carry large plastic or net bags in which to collect small items. To lift heavy objects to the surface, workers utilize chains and ropes that are attached to pulleys on support boats.

Another lifting method involves the use of air bags. Workers use ropes to attach heavy artifacts to air bags, which look like small hot-air balloons. As the air bag rises to the surface, the water pressure decreases, causing the small amount of compressed air within the bag to expand. Archaeologists usually use several air bags to lift a heavy object to the surface.

Excavators attach air bags to an early cannon to help lift it to the surface.

THE SHIP BENEATH THE CITY

In 1981 a property developer named Howard Ronson applied to the city of New York to construct an office building in lower Manhattan, one of the city's five boroughs. The city required that archaeologists examine the site before any new construction could begin. Located near the East River, which connects to the Atlantic Ocean, the building site had been a parking lot for many years. Beneath the old parking lot, excavators discovered the remains of a 250-year-old trading ship.

Archaeologists determined that in about 1750 workers sank the ship on purpose as part of a landfill project to extend Manhattan Island. Laborers had anchored down the vessel and filled it with sand and rocks. When the expansion project was completed, the ship was underground and two blocks from water.

Known as the Ronson ship, the vessel was 100 feet (30 meters) long and 26 feet (8 m) at its widest point. The merchant ship, which could carry more than 200 tons (181 metric tons), is the only known example of the cargo vessels that sailed the trade routes between Britain, the West Indies, and the North American colonies. Excavators restored the ship's bow (front), which is now on display at the Mariners' Museum in Newport News, Virginia.

Experts repair the timbers of a seventeenth-century ship. Unless it is treated with special chemicals, waterlogged wood can warp, shrink, or crack as it dries.

Preserving the Past

Archaeologists and restorers take many different approaches to removing, transporting, and storing artifacts found underwater. Scientists must first decide whether or not to remove the artifact from its underwater environment. Very fragile materials, such as the wood of an ancient ship, could be destroyed in the air at the surface. In these situations, archaeologists may choose to study the artifact underwater and leave the object where it sank.

Items brought to the surface can be transported in fresh water or in chemical preservatives. In recent years, scientists have experimented with storing ancient objects in gels, which cushion the artifacts. Sometimes very delicate items are placed in specially designed underwater storage pits. These objects will remain in the pits until scientists can develop techniques to safely preserve them on dry land.

Restorers use small hand tools to remove a crusty coating from an artifact.

Layers of encrustation *(right)*
hid the shape and beauty of
this old lantern *(below)*.

THE MEDITERRANEAN SEA: IN SEARCH OF THE PAST

The word *Mediterranean* means "center of the earth." For the ancient people who lived on the shores of the Mediterranean Sea, this almost landlocked body of water was indeed at the center of all things. On the Mediterranean's northern shores are the European nations of Spain, France, Italy, and Greece. The fertile lands of North Africa, including Egypt, Tunisia, Libya, and Morocco, border the sea to the south. To the east, are the Middle Eastern countries of Turkey, Syria, Lebanon, and Israel. At its western edge, the Mediterranean opens to the Atlantic Ocean through the Strait of Gibraltar.

The Mediterranean Sea is tame compared to the open oceans. It has minor tides, mild currents, and gentle winds. Storms are rare and cannot rival the violence of a hurricane or a typhoon. Yet the Mediterranean's storms, when they happen, are dangerous enough. Storm-tossed waves can sometimes reach more than 25 feet (7.6 m).

Blue-green waters wash against the beaches of Cyprus (above), an island in the eastern Mediterranean Sea. For hundreds of years, fishers (right) from southern Europe, North Africa, and the Middle East have cast their nets into the Mediterranean's fish-filled depths.

These waves are tall enough to smash even the largest and strongest ancient vessels.

Ancient people in the Mediterranean built large ships for trade, warfare, and exploration, and they transported money, cargo, and supplies by sea. Thousands of boats crossed the Mediterranean in ancient times, and many of them sank. As a result, the Mediterranean is one of the most important regions for underwater archaeologists. Probably no other body of water has been more heavily traveled. And there is probably no other sea with as many sunken cargoes and wrecks waiting to be discovered and examined.

A Sea of Struggles

Since ancient times, the Mediterranean Sea has connected people of many different cultures. About 3000 B.C., the pharaohs (rulers) of ancient Egypt sent their ships to explore lands beyond the narrow Nile River Valley, where the Egyptian civilization flourished. The great armies of Persia, a kingdom in the

Merchants from Phoenicia, an ancient land on the eastern coast of the Mediterranean Sea, show their wares to the residents of Cyprus. The Phoenicians established the first Mediterranean trading centers in the fifth century B.C.

Ancient Roman warships patrolled the Mediterranean Sea to protect merchant ships from pirates.

Middle East, sailed the Mediterranean to conquer lands to the west.

Later the armies of ancient Greece and Rome traveled eastward to take control of the Middle East. In the twelfth and thirteenth centuries A.D., long after the fall of the Greeks and Romans, Crusaders (Christian armies from western Europe) set out across the Mediterranean to conquer the Holy Land (modern Israel and Jordan).

In the 1300s, the Turks came to rule Asia Minor (modern Turkey) and controlled an important Mediterranean trade route. At the same time, North African pirates robbed European merchant ships that strayed too far from their home ports of Spain, France, and Italy. The Europeans, who traded with India and areas farther east, looked for safer trade routes beyond the Mediterranean. This search eventually led the explorer Christopher Columbus to the Americas in 1492.

During the nineteenth century, the wealthy and powerful nations of western Europe—especially Britain and France—struggled for control of two strategic passages in

During the sixteenth and seventeenth centuries A.D., pirates from the Barbary States of North Africa looted trading ships on the Mediterranean. In 1801 the United States was drawn into war with Tripoli, one of the Barbary States. The U.S. Navy (above) blockaded Tripoli's ports and bombed its cities.

the Mediterranean Sea. The Strait of Gibraltar offers boats a natural exit to the Atlantic Ocean. The artifical Suez Canal, in Egypt, links the Mediterranean Sea with the Red Sea and then with seas farther south and east.

In modern times, the Mediterranean Sea has continued to play a strategic role in world history. The sea was the scene of battles fought during World War I (1914–1918) and World War II (1939–1945). For decades after World War II, a naval rivalry between the United States and the Soviet Union was played out on the Mediterranean Sea.

GUIDING LIGHTS

Lighthouses are towers that beam extremely strong light toward open water. These structures are built at harbors, on peninsulas, or on isolated rocks. Some lighthouses are even anchored to the seafloor. For thousands of years, lighthouses have helped sailors to navigate and have warned ships away from dangerous rocks and reefs.

The ancient Egyptians were probably the first people to guide ships with light by building fires on hills and later by using fire as a light source in their first lighthouses. In the third century B.C., the Egyptians constructed the Pharos of Alexandria, the tallest lighthouse ever made. This structure directed ships for 1,500 years.

Modern lighthouses project light through special lenses that increase the intensity of a lamp. The Fresnel lense, for example, is equipped with triangular prisms that break up light. With this lense, the lamp's light can be seen more than 20 miles (32 kilometers) out to sea.

Most lighthouses send out identifiable patterns of light called characteristics. Some characteristics are flashing lights, while others are steady beams. During a journey, sailors consult lists of lighthouse characteristics to de-termine their ship's location. Many lighthouses are also equipped with radio beacons, which send radio signals to nearby vessels.

Since the 1940s, the number of lighthouses has decreased with the improvement of electronic navigation. As a result, only about 1,400 lighthouses are currently in use on the world's waterways. Many lighthouses are now historical sites where people can learn about seafaring and can view the workings of lamps and lenses.

Peter Throckmorton (left) and George Bass (right) led the first scientific excavation of an underwater site.

Pioneering Work

Scientists once believed that submerged wrecks should be quickly brought to the surface and studied on dry land. This attitude began to change in the 1960s, when archaeologists working in the Mediterranean Sea proved that technical excavation could be done deep underwater. At that time, divers used careful excavation methods to uncover a shipwreck at Cape Gelidonya off the coast of southern Turkey.

The leaders of the Gelidonya operation were Peter Throckmorton, a journalist, photographer, and diver, and archaeologist George Bass, both from the United States. Pursuing a longtime interest in underwater archaeology, Throck-morton and Bass organized an international team of scientists to excavate a 3,000-year-old shipwreck.

The goal of the Gelidonya archaeologists was not to recover a lot of artifacts but to learn about the ancient site and about the people who had sailed the ancient ship. No object was brought to the surface before its exact location was recorded. Working layer by layer, excavators sketched each item before lifting it to the surface. Wood and metal objects were successfully removed, reconstructed, repaired, and preserved for future generations.

After excavating the site, the archaeologists were able to piece together the story of the Gelidonya shipwreck. They believed that the

An international team of archaeologists excavated the wreck of a 3,000-year-old merchant ship off the rugged coast of Cape Gelidonya (right). During the excavation, divers discovered a variety of bronze tools (below).

crew had sailed northwestward from Syria to the Aegean region between Greece and Turkey. At Cape Gelidonya, the ship ran into a group of jagged rocks and sank in nearly 90 feet (27 m) of water.

On board were pieces of copper and bronze, as well as metalworking tools. The cargo suggested to the archaeologists that, between ports, the crew hammered, pol-ished, and sharpened metal objects. Personal items, such as jewelry and religious artifacts, showed that the ship was from Phoenicia. This region now includes the coastal areas of Syria, Lebanon, and Israel. Dated to about 1200 B.C., the wreck proved that the Phoenicians were trading in the Mediterranean region much earlier than historians had originally believed.

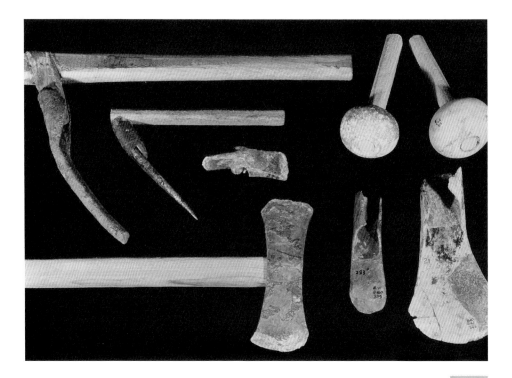

SHIPWRECKS AND SCIENCE

Divers have discovered hundreds of shipwrecks throughout the world since the pioneering work of Peter Throckmorton and George Bass. Further excavations in the Mediterranean Sea—as well as work in the Indian Ocean, the Pacific Ocean, the North Atlantic Ocean, and the Caribbean Sea—have yielded important information about ancient shipbuilding and trade.

Mediterranean Wrecks

Near the southern coast of Turkey lies the island of Yassi Ada. Jutting out from the island is a dangerous reef, which in some places is less than 6 feet (1.8 meters) below the surface. Near the reef, divers have discovered the visible remains of more than a dozen ships ranging in date from the third century B.C. to the 1930s.

From 1961 to 1964, an archaeological team excavated the remains of a seventh-century Byzantine merchant ship near Yassi Ada. The Byzantine Empire once ruled much of southeastern Europe and the Middle East. The ship carried more than 900 amphorae (clay storage jars) for transporting wine, olive oil, and other goods. Excavators brought about 100 of these jars to the surface.

After the ship itself was cleared of mud, sand, and other debris, the sea current began to loosen bits of wood, which then floated away. To solve this problem, the team used about 2,000 bicycle spokes to pin each remaining piece of wood to the seafloor until the entire ship could be drawn and recorded.

Eventually, restorers reassembled the remaining pieces of the ship on land. From this reconstruction, archaeologists learned not only the exact size and shape of the boat but also the methods that ancient Byzantine shipbuilders had used. The excavation at Yassi Ada greatly expanded archaeologists' knowledge of how waterlogged wood survives and how it can be recovered and preserved.

Archaeologists learned even more about recovering wooden ships in the late 1960s when a

A diver surveys a ship resting on the seafloor.

group of U.S. archaeologists excavated the wreck of a Greek merchant ship dating to the fourth century B.C. The vessel sank near the port of Kyrenia on the island of Cyprus. At the time of excavation, archaeologists knew little about the construction and design of ancient Greek merchant ships.

Excavators spent eight years recording every detail of the ship, raising it to the surface, and reassembling the pieces. Now on display in Kyrenia Castle, this ship is one of the best-preserved ancient Greek vessels. Workers built an exact copy of the ship in 1985. Named the *Kyrenia II,* the ship was sailed from Athens to Cyprus in 1986.

More recent discoveries in the Mediterranean Sea have revealed a great deal about ancient maritime traffic and trade. Many archaeologists consider the Ulu Burun wreck—which divers found off the

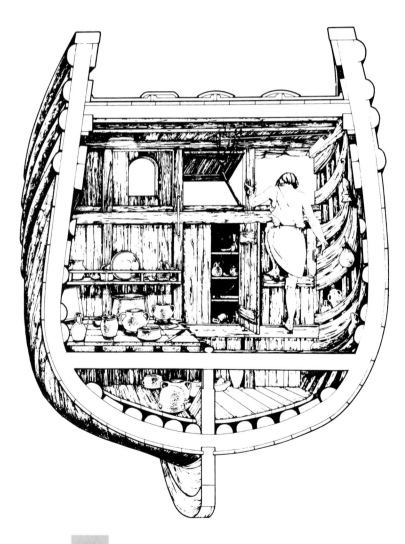

Artifacts and data were collected during the excavation of an ancient ship at Yassi Ada near Turkey. From this information, an artist rendered a drawing of how the vessel's stern (rear section) might have looked.

An archaeologist excavates the hull (body) of a ship near the port of Kyrenia, Cyprus. Dating to the fourth century B.C., the Kyrenia wreck contained tall amphorae (left) and heavy, square millstones (right), which were probably used to weigh down and steady the ship during its journey.

coast of southern Turkey in 1983— to be the most spectacular ancient shipwreck ever discovered.

Dating to the fourteenth century B.C., this boat sailed along the east- ern shore of the Mediterranean and carried a wide variety of cargo. Archaeologists discovered pottery from Cyprus, flasks from Syria, jewelry, metalworking tools, and

A diver examines pottery from the Ulu Burun shipwreck off the coast of southern Turkey. Silver jewelry, pieces of ivory, and glass beads also made up part of the treasure recovered from this wreck, which dates to the fourteenth century B.C.

hundreds of copper bars. This wreck revealed much about the flow of goods in the Mediterranean region.

In the late 1980s, excavators explored two other shipwrecks that indicated the extent of trade in the Mediterranean. Found near the Italian island of Giglio, a merchant ship dating to 600 B.C. held decorative pottery from at least six different locations. The boat's cargo also included shipbuilding tools, weapons, furniture, fishing gear, and copper and lead bars. Archaeologists believe the Giglio vessel was a competitive trading ship that sailed an established route.

In contrast, the Dattilo wreck, which divers found near the Italian island of Panarea, carried only fine pottery. The cargo, which dates to the fifth century B.C., consisted almost entirely of black painted cups, beakers, plates, jugs, bowls, and oil lamps. The Dattilo wreck provided archaeologists with the earliest evidence of bulk cargoes, which showed that merchants and their suppliers were beginning to specialize.

Asian Shipwrecks

Commerce flourished in the Indian Ocean during the sixth century A.D., when a brisk trade developed between the Arabian Peninsula and India. Overland trade routes brought goods from the Mediterranean Sea across the peninsula to the Arabian coast. Merchants transported this cargo across the Arabian Sea to India. By traveling eastward from India, trading ships could reach ports in Southeast Asia, China, and Japan, all of which were linked to the Pacific Ocean. Asian merchants sailed westward with cargoes of carpets, gold, silver, pearls, silk, pottery, and perfume.

The Chinese, who did not have oceangoing ships until the eighth century, began to copy the designs of visiting vessels. By the late 900s, Chinese shipbuilders had perfected their skills. In 1973 archaeologists

Painted on a large screen, this scene depicts an early merchant ship anchored near a Japanese port. Small boats, which can maneuver through shallow water, bring the goods to shore.

In the wreck of a thirteenth-century ship near the port of Quanzhou in eastern China, archaeologists discovered cowrie shells (left) and tortoise shells (below). Many Asian cultures once used these items as money.

excavated an early Chinese ship found near the port of Quanzhou on China's eastern coast. The ship, which dates to 1277, was carrying a vast and varied load. The vessel's main cargo was 2 tons (1.8 metric tons) of fragrant wood, including sandalwood and eaglewood. Divers also collected cowrie shells, tortoise shells, and fine pottery.

Seated beneath a canopy, a Dutch admiral and the ruler of a kingdom on the Indonesian island of Java negotiate a trade agreement.

The Quanzhou wreck tested archaeologists' knowledge of Chinese shipbuilding. Before the discovery of the Quanzhou site, for example, scholars believed that the ancient Chinese had always built flat-bottomed boats similar to many of China's modern vessels. The Quanzhou vessel, however, had a distinct *V* shape, with the lower sides tapering inward to a long, heavy keel (a central beam that runs along the bottom of a ship). The keel helped to keep the vessel steady in rough seas. Since its discovery, the Quanzhou ship has helped archaeologists see how the pieces of other Chinese wrecks might fit together.

In the 1600s, European trading companies sent large fleets to the Indian and Pacific oceans. Stopping at ports throughout Asia, crews traded silver for a wide variety of goods. Strong winds and violent storms, however, made these sea voyages treacherous and sank many trading ships. So far, divers have found about 25 of the European trading ships in these oceans. But historical records show that hundreds more were lost.

The English warship **Mary Rose** *went down during a battle against France in 1545. The heavily armed vessel carried bronze cannons, guns, and bows and arrows for close-range fighting.*

One of the most famous wrecks, the *Batavia*, belonged to the Dutch East India Company and went down in 1629. According to the journal of the *Batavia's* commander, the ship was wrecked 40 miles (64 km) off the western coast of Australia.

Divers found the *Batavia's* remains in a coral reef, protected from the pounding surf. They brought many large, sandstone blocks to the surface. From historical documents, archaeologists learned that the *Batavia* was taking

the blocks to the port of Batavia (modern Jakarta on the Indonesian island of Java). The blocks were meant to frame the entrance to the Dutch East India Company's headquarters. In 1979 restorers used these blocks to reconstruct the gateway for the Western Australia Maritime Museum in Fremantle.

European Warships

Using large navies, the sixteenth-century kingdoms of Europe fought

Workers (below) restore the waterlogged hull of the Mary Rose, *which was brought to the surface in 1982. Underwater archaeologists recovered many of the crew's personal items (right), including a comb, some coins, and a set of rosary beads.*

their opponents at sea. These warships carried cannons, guns, and other weapons fired with gun powder. Many of the vessels sank during battle, while some went down without having fired a shot. The excavation of two European war vessels has helped archaeolo-gists understand how the Europeans fought and lived at sea.

In 1545 the English king Henry VIII watched from shore as one of his most important warships sank during a battle against France. The *Mary Rose* and its crew of 700 sailors went down in the Solent, a

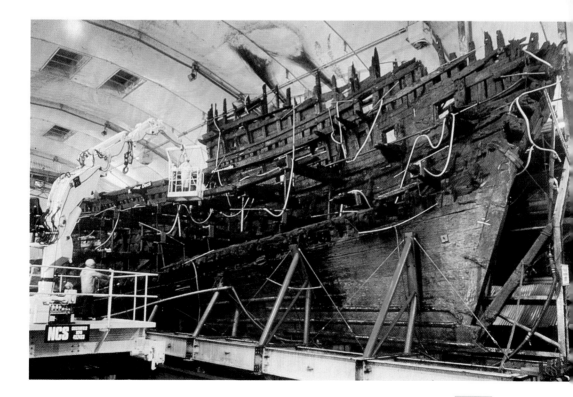

narrow channel between mainland England and the small Isle of Wight. Fewer than 40 people escaped from the wreck, which settled into the soft mud of the Solent, buried intact beneath silt and debris.

In 1979 a team of archaeologists and other specialists began excavating the contents of the *Mary Rose.* Divers brought up 15 cannons and more than 100 guns, as well as ammunition. Through excavation, archaeologists gained valuable information about the construction and organization of one of Henry VIII's greatest battleships. In 1982 the ship was successfully floated to the surface.

The raising of the *Vasa,* a Swedish warship, was one of the largest and most thorough excavations ever undertaken by maritime archaeologists. Built to be the flagship of the Swedish navy, the *Vasa*

In 1961 a specially constructed frame floated the Swedish warship Vasa *to Stockholm's harbor, a short distance from where the vessel sank during its first voyage in 1628.*

Dhows have sailed the Arab waterways for many centuries.

ARAB TRADE WINDS

Strong seasonal winds called monsoons blow across the Indian Ocean. To take advantage of these winds, ancient shipbuilders from the Arabian Peninsula designed dhows, ships that were specially constructed to withstand rough seas and the gusts of monsoons. Workers made the earliest dhows by lashing together timbers with rope. The ropes were covered with oils to help preserve them in the sea.

Strong enough to carry heavy cargoes—including elephants— Arab dhows followed the wind patterns to eastern Africa, India, China, and other lands that bordered the Indian Ocean. During December and January, for example, merchants sailed south, bringing horses, salt, and textiles to African ports. In April and May, dhows carrying gold and ivory returned to Arabia pushed by winds blowing from the southwest. Modern Arabian traders still navigate the Indian Ocean using both traditional and motorized dhows.

left Stockholm's harbor on its first voyage in 1628. Less than .5 miles (.8 km) from shore, the ship was caught in a sudden gust of wind, tipped, and quickly sunk. Immediate attempts to raise the ship failed.

In 1956 divers discovered the *Vasa* upright and almost completely intact. Some excavators brought up the contents of the ship, while others dug tunnels underneath it to prepare the vessel for transport to the surface. Divers passed steel

Workers clean and repair the **Vasa's lower gun deck** *(above).* **A restorer holds a ring** *(left),* **the only gold artifact found during excavation of the royal warship.**

wires through the tunnels to make a lifting cradle. Eventually, the *Vasa* was towed to shallow water where restorers repaired and strengthened the ship. In 1961 the *Vasa* was raised and floated to dry land.

Caribbean Finds

During the 1500s, Spanish ships crossed the Atlantic to explore and conquer land in North and South America. The most traveled area

A diver uses an airlift to remove spoil from the Molasses Reef site in the Caribbean Sea. The sixteenth-century Spanish vessel that sank here is the oldest shipwreck yet discovered in the Caribbean region.

was the Caribbean Sea, a large body of water between North and South America in which numerous islands are located.

A largely enclosed sea, the Caribbean has several passages linking it to sea-lanes in the Atlantic. Early navigators who entered the Caribbean through eastern passages found that strong east-to-west winds made a return journey along the same route difficult. Instead, ships returning to the Atlantic Ocean sailed northward past dangerous underwater reefs. Because of these hazards, the Caribbean holds a number of shipwrecks.

The oldest Caribbean shipwreck yet found is a Spanish vessel dating to the early sixteenth century. Divers discovered the site, known as the Molasses Reef, north of the island of Hispaniola, which is shared by the countries of Haiti and the Dominican Republic. Sailing northwestward, the ship sank after striking a reef. The ship's cargo, which included weapons and ammunition, littered the seafloor 20 feet (6 m) below the surface.

An archaeologist inspects ballast (heavy materials) found aboard a Spanish ship that sank at Highborn Cay in the Bahamas, an island group located southeast of Florida. Sailors commonly weighted their vessels with ballast to steady the boats.

Excavators at Highborn Cay uncover a ship's main mast-step, a framework that anchors the mast. A long pole that rises from the deck of a ship, the mast carries the vessel's sails.

In 1982 archaeologists began a systematic excavation of the Molasses Reef wreck. Divers recovered many different kinds of artillery, as well as molds for making ammunition, which archaeologists believe the crew produced while at sea.

In the same year, excavators started surveying a wreck at Highborn Cay in the Bahamas. This site also held a sixteenth-century Spanish ship with a cargo of weapons and ammunition. Archaeologists conducted underwater studies of the well-preserved ship in 1983 and in 1986 and have since left the site undisturbed. From the wreck, archaeologists have gained valuable information about the construction of early Spanish ships.

RUINED HARBORS
AND SUNKEN CITIES

Before the development of cities and seaports, sailors anchored and unloaded their boats in bays and at the mouths of rivers. These natural harbors could shelter the small, open boats of ancient times, many of which could be dragged out of the water in rough weather.

As trade increased, however, people began building larger boats that natural harbors could not accommodate. The boats required protection from the waves of the open sea. The vessels also needed to be anchored in deep water to prevent running aground. Merchant ships, in particular, required a place to anchor where goods could be unloaded directly onto dry land.

Phoenician Harbors

The earliest harbors of Phoenicia satisfied most maritime needs. The docks had walls that offered protection from the open sea and small areas where the water was deep enough for a large ship to anchor. Some early Phoenician harbors also had storehouses, where goods could be kept safe and dry.

As maritime trade increased, many port cities built inland boat basins. A boat basin was like a huge swimming pool, with an entrance leading to it from the open sea. The land around the boat basin was usually flat—and often paved—so that workers could easily load or unload ships tied to the dock.

The Phoenicians, who had large trading fleets, built boat basins at their ports throughout the Mediterranean. One of the largest of these ports was at Carthage in modern Tunisia, North Africa. The complex harbor at Carthage sheltered not only Phoenician merchant ships but also warships that protected the traders.

The Carthage harbor consisted of three parts—a breakwater, an outer basin, and an inner basin. The breakwater was a long wall that ran parallel to the coastline. Ships anchored between the breakwater and the shore were safe from storms, reefs, and waves. This breakwater also acted as a pier onto which cargo could be loaded and unloaded when the sea was calm.

Carthage allowed ships of foreign nations to use the breakwater, but only Carthaginian ships could enter the protected basins. Merchant ships anchored in the outer basin,

In 1755 a powerful wave called a tsunami destroyed the city of Lisbon, Portugal, which lies along the coast of the Atlantic Ocean. Tsunamis are caused by the eruption of underwater volcanoes or by earthquakes on the ocean floor.

which was roughly oval in shape. From the outer basin, warships traveled through a short channel to a smaller inner basin, which was shaped like a doughnut. In the center stood a building that housed the military command of the Carthaginian navy.

The Harbors of Ancient Greece

Like the Phoenicians, the ancient Greeks recognized the importance of well-built harbors to maintain merchant vessels and warships. The Greeks also needed to fortify their harbors against sea raids.

Gentle waves wash against the ruins of Atlit, an ancient Phoenician port. Ships unloaded their goods at Atlit's wharf (foreground) and were sheltered from the open sea by a long wall called a breakwater (background).

SHIPS PAST AND PRESENT

The first boat was probably just a log on which a rider sat while paddling across a river or a lake. Ancient people later learned how to tie logs together to make rafts and how to dig out a log to fashion a canoe. About 3000 B.C., the ancient Egyptians began building boats with wood frameworks and wood planking. Early Egyptian shipbuilders discovered that upright sails placed on poles perpendicular to the boat could harness the wind. These innovations helped ancient people construct large trading vessels and warships.

For thousands of years, shipbuilders worked to develop bigger and faster ships. Early sails were square and, when raised, crossed the width of a ship. Square sails were most effective when the wind blew in from behind the sail. To help a ship maneuver into the wind, builders invented lateen, or triangular, sails. Sailors placed lateen sails along the length of a ship. Using ropes to turn the sails, lateens could catch the wind from any direction.

By the A.D. 1400s, a combination of square and lateen sails powered what was called a full-rigged ship. Full-rigged ships had three sails held by masts (poles).

This sixteenth-century Norwegian ship used a square sail to catch the wind.

The foremast in the front of the ship and the mainmast in the middle held square sails, while the mizzenmast in the rear of the ship supported a lateen sail. Clipper ships, developed in the mid-1800s, were designed for speed, holding a mixture of as many as 35 square and lateen sails.

Most modern oceangoing vessels are now powered by engines, and many ships are automated. For instance, electronic equipment controls the flow of fuel and can often navigate the ship. Since the invention of the airplane, few people travel long distances on ships. Oceans and seas are mostly navigated by enormous cargo vessels that carry goods to all parts of the world. For economic reasons, modern shipbuilders strive to design fast ships that can be easily loaded and unloaded.

Steep cliffs along the Greek coast rise up from the Mediterranean Sea. In ancient times, small boats sought shelter in protected inlets along the Greek shoreline.

A sixteenth-century fortress overlooks the harbor at Iraklion on the Greek island of Crete. Soldiers at the fortress protected this busy port from pirates and other invaders.

For this reason, they built seawalls across the entrances to their harbors, leaving only narrow openings through which ships could pass.

The first such seawalls were very simple. On the Greek island of Delos, for example, workers simply piled up large blocks of stone to make a massive wall. Eventually, the Greeks copied Phoenician techniques and built stronger seawalls.

When divers explored a harbor on the North African coast that the ancient Greeks built, they discovered that the harbor had been constructed in several stages as Greek knowledge and skills had improved. First, the Greeks built a seawall of rough stones to shelter the harbor from the open sea. The area inland from the harbor was then enlarged. Next, heavy piers and shipyards were built out into the water. In the last stage, the harbor was divided into inner and outer sections to make it easier to defend.

Archaeologists explored a similar ancient harbor on the Greek mainland. Over time, the rising sea had submerged the harbor's storerooms and houses. Huge amounts of debris had washed into the ruin. After excavators cleared away the mud, they discovered ancient furniture in some of the buildings. They also found floors that were decorated with mosaics (pictures made with small pieces of material held together with cement).

King Herod's Harbor

During the first century B.C., King Herod ruled Judaea (now southern Israel). He wanted to build up the commercial strength of his kingdom by improving the transport of goods. To achieve this goal, Herod ordered the port of Caesarea to be built on the eastern coast of the Mediterranean.

According to ancient writings, workers lowered huge blocks of stone into water 120 feet (37 m) deep. Each of these stone blocks, which formed the foundation of the harbor facilities, was roughly the size of a modern bus. When the foundation reached the surface of the water, laborers built a pier on top of it that was about 200 feet (61 m) wide and .5 miles (.8 km) long.

Half of the pier served as a break-water to protect the harbor from waves. The other half supported a massive curved wall that enclosed the harbor. Towers were erected along this wall, and a row of arched

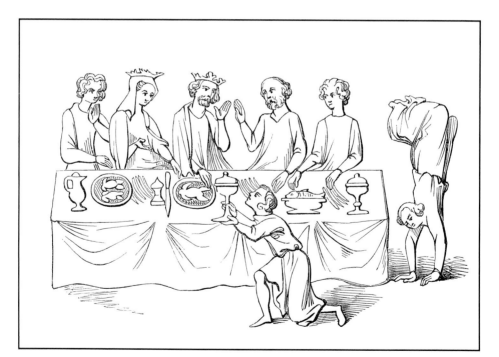

To improve trade between his kingdom and other Mediterranean settlements, King Herod (center) *of Judaea ordered the construction of the port of Caesarea in the first century B.C. Archaeologists believe that earthquakes gradually sank Caesarea's ancient harbor.*

While under British rule, Port Royal on the Caribbean island of Jamaica developed into a thriving pirate headquarters. An earthquake that struck Port Royal in 1692 sank two-thirds of the city.

shelters served as a resting place for foreign crews.

Because little evidence of the ancient harbor existed, experts believed this ancient description of Caesarea was greatly exaggerated. In 1960, however, a U.S. team of underwater archaeologists explored the site and were astounded by the size of Herod's harbor. The port's dimensions were just as the ancient writings described. Experts have now determined that earthquakes gradually tumbled Caesarea's harbor into the sea.

Port Royal

Located on the southern coast of the island of Jamaica, Port Royal was once one of the most prosperous seaports in the Caribbean. Throughout the 1600s, the city was the crowded home of merchants, missionaries, smugglers, pirates, and drifters. At the height of its prosperity, Port Royal was populated by more than 6,500 people. About 2,000 buildings, many of which were several stories tall, lined the city's narrow streets.

In 1692 an earthquake destroyed two-thirds of Port Royal. Two thousand people were killed instantly, and 3,000 more died of injuries and disease soon after the disaster. A large portion of the port sank 65 feet (20 m) below sea level and could be seen dimly through the water. The remainder of the city was heavily damaged.

Full-scale excavation of Port Royal did not begin until 1966, when the Jamaican government considered dredging the site for a modern port. A team of divers spent more than two years recovering thousands of artifacts, including household utensils, coins, tools, weapons, and pieces of fine pewter.

In 1981 a field school was established at Port Royal. Using seventeenth-century maps, these excavators are exploring the underwater city layer by layer. Experts predict that it will take decades to complete the study of Port Royal, which is one of the most important archaeological sites in the world.

After the destruction of Port Royal (above), *workers began to rebuild. Other disasters, such as fires and hurricanes, however, plagued the city, and Port Royal was never reestablished as a trading center.*

Excavators have recovered a variety of pewter items (above) from Port Royal, including plates, bowls, utensils, and candleholders. Many of the city's remains, such as the walls and floors of buildings (right), are still being explored by underwater archaeologists.

THE MYSTERY OF ATLANTIS

In the fourth century B.C., the Greek philospher Plato described the legend of Atlantis in his writings. According to Plato, Atlantis was once an island nation that supported a great civilization. The inhabitants of the island, which had bountiful natural resources, were known as skilled artists and architects. But the people of Atlantis became corrupt and greedy, and the gods decided to punish them. After a day and night of violent earthquakes and floods, Atlantis sank into the sea and was never seen again.

Archaeologists and historians have offered numerous theories for the mystery of Atlantis. Most scholars, however, believe Atlantis was actually Thera, a Greek island in the Aegean Sea. The Minoans—a cultured people known for their beautiful pottery, jewelry, and paintings—once lived on Thera and on the neighboring island of Crete. The people of these two islands prospered from maritime trade.

During the mid-1400s B.C., however, powerful volcanic eruptions caused Thera to collapse into the sea. These disasters occurred at the same time as the decline of the Minoan civilization. The sudden disappearance of both Thera and the civilization that thrived there led scholars to link this story to the legend of Atlantis.

An artist's depiction of the lost continent of Atlantis shows fish swimming among the ruins of columned buildings.

Two archaeologists videotape a site using a light and an underwater camera. Video cameras are most useful for recording the progress of an excavation and for briefing divers on the status of a project.

The Future of Underwater Archaeology

In the past, accidental discoveries by local divers and by fishing crews led archaeologists to valuable finds. Modern scientists have come to rely almost completely on their own survey techniques to locate sites stuck in thick mud or sunk in deep water. Less than 50 years ago, archaeologists simply studied objects that divers took from the sea bottom. Scientists now demand

Many archaeologists are beginning to focus on wrecks located in rivers and lakes. To search these areas, divers sometimes use waterproof metal detectors *(left)*. To study objects in very deep water, scientists lower ROVs *(below)*, which can be equipped with mechanical arms to collect samples from the seafloor.

that underwater excavations be carried out carefully and precisely. These experts want to ensure that, as underwater remains are removed from the sea, as much information as possible is preserved.

Underwater archaeology is a young science, but it is making rapid progress with the help of many experts. Oceanographers, geologists, and other scientists have just begun to develop the techniques and skills needed to search the mountains and caverns of the ocean floor. In the future, these advanced exploration methods will help underwater archaeologists locate the thousands of sites that have been far beyond the reach of divers. From these finds, and from the information they contain, we will have even more clues about how people lived, traveled, and traded in the past.

A geologist drills into the depth of coral encrustation to take a core sample. By analyzing the coral's annual layers of growth, the scientist will be able to estimate when the site's remains sank. This dating method is called sclerochronology.

PRONUNCIATION GUIDE

Batavia (buh-TAY-vee-uh)

Caesarea (see-zuh-REE-uh)

Gelidonya (gehl-uh-DOH-nyuh)

Gibraltar (juh-BRAWL-tuhr)

Giglio (JEEL-yoh)

Kyrenia (kih-REE-nyuh)

Phoenicia (fih-NEESH-uh)

Suez (soo-EHZ)

Vasa (VAH-sah)

Archaeologists unearth the remains of a nineteenth-century fishing boat. Blown ashore during a storm, the vessel was buried beneath the sands of an island off the coast of South Carolina.

GLOSSARY

airlift: a tool used to suck up earth, rocks, and vegetation. The airlift consists of a long tube attached to an air compressor on a support vessel.

archaeologist: a scientist who studies the material remains of past human life.

artifact: any object made by a human. Artifacts can include items crafted from natural materials, such as bone, stone, clay, or wood.

bacteria: one-celled living beings that can only be seen through a microscope. Thousands of different kinds of bacteria exist. Some, for example, cause diseases, while others help break up chemicals.

encrustation: the formation of a crusty layer on the surface of an object.

excavate: to dig up and remove objects from an archaeological site.

remotely operated vehicle (ROV): a robot that moves in response to human or computer commands given from a distance. ROVs can send video images to scientists on the surface, and some machines can gather samples with mechanical arms.

salvager: a person who recovers objects from something that has been damaged or destroyed, such as a sunken ship.

A small clown fish rests within the tentacles of a giant sea anemone. Underwater archaeologists encounter many different kinds of animals on the seafloor.

scuba: a piece of equipment worn by divers for breathing under water. Scuba gear includes an air tank connected by a hose to a mouthpiece.

sonar: a device that sends sound waves through the water and records the returning echoes. The echoes bounce off objects on the seafloor and appear as lines on paper.

spoil: earth, rock, and vegetation excavated from an archaeological site.

swimline: a survey method in which a group of divers spreads out in a straight line and swims together in the same direction to observe the seafloor.

towed search: a survey technique in which a boat pulls a diver on a board called a sled. By pressing controls on the sled, surveyors can adjust their distance from the seafloor.

INDEX

An archaeologist photographs ship timbers recovered from a river site in South Carolina.

Workers raise one of the anchors found aboard the wreck of the Swedish warship Vasa.

Photo Acknowledgments

© John D. Brooks Photography, pp. 2, 15, 23, 39; Paul Caputo, Quiescence Diving Services, Key Largo, Florida, p. 7; Florida State Archives, p. 8; Meredith Pillon/Greek National Tourist Organization, p. 9; Dave B. Fleetham/Visuals Unlimited, p. 10; South Carolina Institute of Archaeology and Anthropology, pp. 12, 66 (top), 68, 70; Jamaican Tourist Board, p. 13; Laura Westlund, p. 16; © Ships of Discovery, pp. 17 (top), 18, 25, 51, 52, 53, 67; Don Frey/INA, pp. 17 (bottom), 21, 36 (right), 37 (bottom), 42; INA, pp. 22, 37 (top); National Park Service, p. 19 (top); National Park Service/photo by Dan Lenihan, p. 19 (bottom); © Lt. Commander R. W. Critch, U.S. Navy, p. 20; Harley J. Seeley/Michigan Maritime Museum, p. 24; The Mariners' Museum, Newport News, Virginia, p. 26; Mary Rose Trust, pp. 11, 27, 28, 29 (top and bottom), 46, 47 (top and bottom); © Andrew E. Beswick, p. 31 (top and bottom); Independent Picture Service, pp. 32, 33, 40, 41, 48, 49, 56, 61, 62; U.S. Navy, p. 34; Voscar, The Maine Photographer, p. 35; Jan Witte, Nova University Oceanographic Center, p. 36 (left); Asian Art Museum of San Francisco, p. 43; William E. Daehn, p. 44 (top); Minneapolis Public Library and Information Center, p. 44 (bottom); James Ford Bell Library, University of Minnesota, p. 45; The Vasa Museum, pp. 50 (top and bottom), 71; The Mansell Collection, pp. 55, 60; Library of Congress, p. 57; Bruce Berg/Visuals Unlimited, p. 58; Daniel H. Condit, p. 59; Donny Hamilton/Texas A & M, p. 63 (top and bottom); Ron Miller, p. 64; National Park Service/photo by John D. Brooks, p. 65; Woods Hole Oceanographic Institution, p. 66 (bottom); John Clifton, p. 69.

Cover photographs: The Vasa Museum (front) and National Park Service/Photo by John D. Brooks (back).